DECEMBER 1 ★ THURSDAY OF THE FIRST WEEK
ISAIAH 26:1-6; MATTHEW 7:21, 24-27

Only a test

"Everyone who listens to these words of mine and acts on them will be like a wise man who built his house on rock." MATTHEW 7:24

It's quite a moment to watch the solid walls of your home shaking like a cardboard popcorn box getting knocked over in a movie theater. But that's what happens when you live in earthquake country, where my family lives. Every home and family has its share of terrifying potential disasters. But no family—no matter how churchgoing, loving, and attentive we are—can escape trials. So we all need regular emergency drills: Pray together. Receive the sacraments. Talk about God with your kids. Read the Bible and stories of saints to them. This is how you stay strong even if everything crumbles around you.

FAMILY PRAYER

Parent: Lord God, bless our home and family.
  All: Open the door to my heart, Lord.
Parent: Make our dwelling a light-house: a place
    where you can live.
  All: Open the door to my heart, Lord.
Parent: Bless with your light and peace all who enter here.
  All: Open the door to my heart, Lord. Amen.

(Invite everyone to share a favorite memory from the past year.)

ADVENT ACTION

Devote a place in your home for everyone to gather in prayer. Make it comfortable and prayerful, with a Bible, crucifix, candle, rosary beads, or whatever is important to your family.

DECEMBER 2 ★ FRIDAY OF THE FIRST WEEK

ISAIAH 29:17-24; MATTHEW 9:27-31

Throwback day

Those who find fault shall receive instruction.
Isaiah 29:24

With two teenagers I have many opportunities to look back over our times together. And what do I see? Mistakes. I've made some doozies over the years. Sometimes I convince myself that something I did on a particular day when my son was five will ruin him forever. Parenting mistakes are easy to latch onto, especially because they don't just concern us: they affect this small person we cherish and have responsibility for. We can let our faults and sins rule us. But God doesn't want us to do that. God can help us face our mistakes squarely and move on. Those who find fault in ourselves need to learn—sometimes again and again—that we can find forgiveness, healing, and love in God's own son, Jesus. We just have to ask.

FAMILY PRAYER

Parent: Lord God, none of us is perfect.
    All: Forgive us, Lord.
Parent: When we mess up, Lord, help us admit it.
    All: Forgive us, Lord.
Parent: Help us find your peace, healing, and love.
    All: Forgive us, Lord. Amen.

(Pray together in silence, asking God to forgive you for times you have failed him.)

ADVENT ACTION

Find out when your parish offers confession or an Advent penance service. Mark it on your calendar as a family event you can't miss.

NOVEMBER 27 ★ FIRST SUNDAY OF ADVENT

ISAIAH 2:1-5; ROMANS 13:11-14; MATTHEW 24:37-44

Wake with the Son

"It is the hour now for you to awake from sleep." ROMANS 13:11

It's now two days since Black Friday, and if you were up before dawn searching for good deals, I hope you've caught up on your sleep. Because today is the day to really wake up—to God's presence in your family. God is with you in all you do. So how will you be attentive to him? How will you let him strengthen you through these holidays and holy days and for the rest of your life? How will you make his amazing love present for your children? Now is the time! Wake up to the Son, who lived, died, and rose for you, and you'll be refreshed and ready for anything.

FAMILY PRAYER

Parent: It's time to wake up and walk with the Lord.
    All: Walk in the light of the Lord!
Parent: Lord, let your light guide us every day of our lives.
    All: Walk in the light of the Lord!
Parent: Lord, always point us toward you.
    All: Walk in the light of the Lord! Amen.

(Light one candle on your Advent wreath if you have one. Invite everyone to share how they will walk in God's light this week.)

ADVENT ACTION

Take a walk with your family. Together, look for signs of God's creation preparing for the darkness of winter.

NOVEMBER 28 ★ MONDAY OF THE FIRST WEEK
ISAIAH 4:2-6; MATTHEW 8:5-11

Child proof

"And I say to one, 'Go,' and he goes; and to another, 'Come here,' and he comes..." **Matthew 8:9**

Wouldn't it be great to be like the centurion? You'd only have to say "Go clean your room" once. But instead, God made us like, well, us. And he made kids to be the kind of people who follow our example more than our orders. Which means we have to continually be the people we want our children to be. What is that for you and your kids? We're not talking about their success in school or career. We're talking about who they are. And who we are. We are children of a good and loving God. How are we living proof that we are made in God's image? What "habits of good" do we actively pursue that show our kids who we strive to be?

FAMILY PRAYER

Parent: Bless us, O Lord, and be with us during Advent.
  All: Come, Lord Jesus.
Parent: Bless us, O Lord, and shine your love on us.
  All: Come, Lord Jesus.
Parent: Bless us, O Lord, all the days of our lives.
  All: Come, Lord Jesus! Amen.

(Bless your children by tracing a small cross with your thumb on their foreheads.)

ADVENT ACTION

Make your Advent family plans. Commit to family prayer and time together every day. Mark it on your calendar if you have to.

NOVEMBER 29 ★ TUESDAY OF THE FIRST WEEK

ISAIAH 11:1-10; LUKE 10:21-24

Hark! Your little angels sing

"For although you have hidden these things from the wise and the learned you have revealed them to the childlike." LUKE 10:21

I saw the first toy ads on TV sometime around Halloween. Annoying, isn't it, how advertisers start on our kids earlier every year? But Advent has been coming in the liturgy since the Ascension last May, when the apostles looked for Jesus' return in glory. And it's fitting that Christmas's approach is heralded through our children. Sure, they may announce it by begging for a light saber or a new phone, but how different is that from our approach to God, in petition for our needs? So what messages from your children do you need to heed this week? Is something—or someone—bothering him? Is she stressed about something? What is Jesus telling you—through your child?

FAMILY PRAYER

Parent: Jesus, help us see you in everyone we meet.
    All: Lord, help us see.
Parent: Help us see your beauty in the poor, hungry, and homeless.
    All: Lord, help us see.
Parent: Help us see your love in the lonely and the brokenhearted.
    All: Lord, help us see. Amen.

(Hold hands and pray silently, asking Jesus to help you see him in others.)

ADVENT ACTION

Have your kids make their Christmas lists—of things they will do for others.

NOVEMBER 30 ★ WEDNESDAY OF THE FIRST WEEK

ROMANS 10:9-18; MATTHEW 4:18-22

Reel love

"Come after me, and I will make you fishers of men."
MATTHEW 4:19

Parents gotta love St. Andrew. He's the brother of St. Peter, but unlike other biblical siblings—Martha and Mary, Jacob and Esau, or Cain and Abel—you never hear Andrew arguing with Peter. In fact, he and Peter were working—together—when Jesus called them. (It's said that like Peter, Andrew considered himself unworthy to die the same way Jesus did, so he asked for an X-shaped cross, or saltire, which now bears his name.) If your children's bickering or competitiveness get out of control this week, pray to St. Andrew for a fisherman's patience and strength.

FAMILY PRAYER *(The St. Andrew Christmas Novena)*

All: Hail and blessed be the hour and the moment in which the Son of God was born of the most pure Virgin Mary at midnight in Bethlehem in the piercing cold. In that hour, vouchsafe, O my God, to hear my prayer and grant my desires through the merits of our Savior Jesus Christ and of his Blessed Mother.

(Say this prayer together every day during Advent.)

ADVENT ACTION

Make flags! Start with a St. Andrew's Cross. Place a strip of first-aid tape diagonally from the top right to the bottom left corner of a piece of blue construction paper. Cross with another strip. Now make your own family flag with symbols you choose!

DECEMBER 3 ★ SATURDAY OF THE FIRST WEEK

ISAIAH 30:19-21, 23-26; MATTHEW 9:35—10:1, 5A, 6-8

Love story

"The harvest is abundant but the laborers are few."
MATTHEW 9:37

On a missionary trip to southern India, St. Francis Xavier discovered that European Christians already living there weren't very good examples of the gospel he was trying to spread. Sound familiar? You work hard raising your kids to be good people, but they see adults in the media acting like spoiled, bad-tempered children. But take heart from this sixteenth-century Jesuit saint who converted more than 30,000 people in his lifetime. His simple secret for getting so much good work done was explained by a companion who once wrote that Francis never seemed to lose his joy, no matter the situation, "simply because he loves everyone."

FAMILY PRAYER

(Based on a Prayer of St. Ignatius of Loyola, friend of Francis Xavier)

All: Lord Jesus Christ, all that we have and love comes from you. We surrender it all to be guided by your will. Your love and your grace are wealth enough for us. Give us these, Lord Jesus, and we ask for nothing more. Amen.

(Say each line of the prayer slowly, and have your kids repeat it after you.)

ADVENT ACTION

Find some new role models for your kids. Together, learn more about the church's newest saints: Teresa of Calcutta, José Sánchez del Río (martyr), Junípero Serra, and Louis and Zélie Martin, the parents of Thérèse of Lisieux.

DECEMBER 4 ★ SECOND SUNDAY OF ADVENT

ISAIAH 11:1-10; ROMANS 15:4-9; MATTHEW 3:1-12

Church (anti) social

Welcome one another, then, as Christ welcomed you, for the glory of God.

ROMANS 15:7

No words trigger more confusion and near panic at Catholic churches than these, often spoken just before Mass begins: "Turn and greet your neighbor." Watch for the confused glances! See the awkward smiles! So I ask you. What is it with us? We have pancake breakfasts and golf tournaments. We even have Catholic schools where our kids can find best friends for life. But ask us to speak with the person next to us and it's like we've forgotten that Christ is in our presence at Mass. Or that we in the assembly are the body of Christ—not a symbol but the real thing. So let's practice today: "Hi, I'm__. How are you doing? How can I pray for you?"

FAMILY PRAYER

Parent: Jesus, when we go to Mass, help us see you in the breaking of the bread.
   All: We love you, Jesus.
Parent: Help us hear you in your holy word.
   All: We love you, Jesus.
Parent: Help us see you present all around us in every person.
   All: We love you, Jesus. Amen.

(Light two candles on your Advent wreath, and pray for peace in our world.)

ADVENT ACTION

Google the words: "Jesus Christ you are my life." Learn and teach this beautiful song to your children.

DECEMBER 5 ★ MONDAY OF THE SECOND WEEK

ISAIAH 35:1-10; LUKE 5:17-26

Eternal time management

*Those whom the L*ORD *has ransomed will return and enter Zion singing, crowned with everlasting joy.* ISAIAH 35:10

St. Thérèse of Lisieux used to warn novices not to fall into the trap of aiming for purgatory as a sort of middle ground that didn't require hard work. She said God wants us to strive toward heaven by overcoming our sins and trusting in his mercy. We know that purgatory is a state of being that purifies us sinful folks for heaven. But will we have the time? We're parents, for goodness sake! We'll need to get to heaven right away, so we can start helping our families still on earth. Let's get to work. Let's turn from sin and trust in God's mercy. Let's aim for heaven—for our kids' sakes, and our own.

FAMILY PRAYER

Parent: Dear God, we have so much to do right now.
   All: Make us ready, Lord.
Parent: We have people to forgive and say we're sorry to.
   All: Make us ready, Lord.
Parent: We have bad habits and sins to work on. Send your grace to help us.
   All: Make us ready, Lord. Amen.

(Discuss the week that's ahead. Find ways to cooperate and share tasks.)

ADVENT ACTION

Find examples of optical illusions on the Internet or in books. Talk with your kids about things that may appear okay but that aren't part of God's plan.

DECEMBER 6 ★ TUESDAY OF THE SECOND WEEK

ISAIAH 40:1-11; MATTHEW 18:12-14

God calling

"It is not the will of your heavenly Father that one of these little ones be lost." MATTHEW 18:14

When they were little, my kids practically shouted their prayers at Mass. Now that they're teens, their mouths clamp shut so tightly I think their jaws must ache by the time Mass is over. I suspect they're at Mass out of obligation, but I have to trust that if they wander away once they're on their own, God will call them back in his time and way. We give God's little lambs all the care we can while they're in our fold, so when they venture into the wide-open pasture, their own experiences can help them navigate. God's grace will guide them. Today, think about God's hopes and plans for your child. Ask God what you can do to further his plan.

FAMILY PRAYER

Parent: Lord, we all have big plans.
 All: Bless us today and tomorrow, Lord.
Parent: We may not know what lies ahead.
 All: Bless us today and tomorrow, Lord.
Parent: But we know that no matter what happens, you love us forever.
 All: Bless us today and tomorrow, Lord. Amen.

(Bless each other with a loving handshake or hug.)

ADVENT ACTION

Celebrate St. Nicholas Day with secret kindnesses. Shop for an elderly neighbor, for instance, donate to an animal shelter, or bake treats for someone special.

DECEMBER 7 ★ WEDNESDAY OF THE SECOND WEEK

ISAIAH 40:25-31; MATTHEW 11:28-30

Helicopter parent

They that hope in the Lord will renew their strength, they will soar as with eagles' wings... **Isaiah 40:31**

My kids and I watched a video of a helicopter landing on the deck of a ship in rough seas. The pilot patiently hovered above the dipping and heaving deck for what seemed like ages, until the exact split second when the ship rose enough for him to gently and expertly touch down. I hoped my kids could see that God is like that with us. When we make mistakes and pitch fits, he doesn't shout at us to quit thrashing around. Instead, he waits patiently, keeping a steady eye on our movements, and giving us opportunities to rise up and soar to him. How does God accompany you when the seas get rough? How do you give your family wings to soar up and meet him?

FAMILY PRAYER

Parent: Lord God, bless all who travel right now.
   All: Lord, keep them safe.
Parent: Guide them so they don't lose their way.
   All: Lord, keep them safe.
Parent: Help them find safety and love at the end of every road.
   All: Lord, keep them safe. Amen.

(Pray in silence for all who are away from home, especially those in military service.)

ADVENT ACTION

Write the names of people who are traveling and place them in your prayer spot. Pray for them throughout the season.

DECEMBER 8 ★ THURSDAY OF THE SECOND WEEK
SOLEMNITY OF THE IMMACULATE CONCEPTION OF THE BLESSED VIRGIN MARY

GENESIS 3:9–15, 20; EPHESIANS 1:3–6, 11–12; LUKE 1:26–38

Birth rite

"I am the handmaid of the Lord. May it be done to me according to your word." LUKE 1:38

My friend Kelly had just brewed a cup of tea and was sitting in her office when the phone rang. It was a hospital chaplain calling to tell her a baby had just been born to a teenage mom who wasn't ready. Kelly barely had time to tell her coworkers she was leaving, but within the hour she and her husband were at the hospital greeting their brand-new baby son. Kelly's coworkers left that mug of tea on her desk for weeks as a remembrance of that joyful moment. How about you? What was it like when you first learned you were going to be a parent? Spend some time with Mary reflecting on those incredible moments today.

FAMILY PRAYER

Parent: Hello, beautiful mother, holy Queen of love!
   All: Ave [AH-vay] Maria, Hail Mary!
Parent: Blessed Mother of God, you are our loving mother too.
   All: Ave Maria, Hail Mary!
Parent: Listen to our prayers and bring them to your Son.
   All: Ave Maria, Hail Mary! Amen.

(Invite everyone to share a prayer intention to bring to Mary.)

ADVENT ACTION

Why not make Mary ornaments for your Christmas tree? Print out pictures of Mary for your kids to color, and mount them on a backing. Attach a loop and place on your tree.

DECEMBER 9 ★ FRIDAY OF THE SECOND WEEK
ISAIAH 48:17-19; MATTHEW 11:16-19

Dancing with the Creator

"It is like children who sit in marketplaces and call to one another, 'We played the flute for you, but you did not dance...'" **Matthew 11:16–17**

I read an article recently about how babies need to be imitated to learn basic perceptions about themselves. So when your baby smiles and you smile back, you're teaching her something about herself. Imitating Jesus isn't something we do for God's benefit, but for ours. It's just good for our souls. Have you ever noticed how truly happy people are who genuinely follow Christ? It's like they're listening to some beautiful music we can't hear. That music plays for all of us; we just need to take a little time to tune our ears. When we prayerfully reflect on God's blessings in our life, we begin to hear those faraway notes. Soon, we can't keep from dancing.

FAMILY PRAYER

Parent: Lord God, every good thing we have is from you.
Open our eyes to your many gifts.
   All: Thank you, God.
Parent: For our family....
   All: Thank you, God.
Parent: For our friends....
   All: Thank you, God. Amen.

(Invite everyone to mention something about a family member that they're thankful for.)

ADVENT ACTION

Remember all those nice things everyone said about each other? Now have everyone write notes or draw pictures showing what they'll do in return.

DECEMBER 10 ★ SATURDAY OF THE SECOND WEEK

SIRACH 48:1–4, 9–11; MATTHEW 17:9A, 10–13

Family reunion

You were taken aloft in a whirlwind of fire, in a chariot with fiery horses.
SIRACH 48:9

Yesterday she was a stranger. Today you connected with her on an ancestry site and discovered you share the same great-grandparents. And, hey, doesn't she have your aunt's eyes? During Advent, we connect with some long-lost ancestors of Jesus and find they're more like us than we realize. Take Elijah the prophet, whose words were "as a flaming furnace." Elijah got blamed for things that weren't his fault and had his moments of weakness. But Elijah's faith in the one God won over the people who worshiped many gods. What can you learn about your own faith from this greatest of prophets?

FAMILY PRAYER

Parent: Dear God, we are all your sons and daughters.
   All: Dear Jesus, Mary, and Joseph, pray for us
Parent: Bless our family on earth: those here and those who are far away.
   All: Dear Jesus, Mary, and Joseph, pray for us
Parent: Bless our family in heaven. Help us remember them always with love
   All: Dear Jesus, Mary, and Joseph, pray for us. Amen.

(Invite everyone to mention one person in the family they'd like to pray for.)

ADVENT ACTION

Collect photos of family members near and far, including those who have died. Make them part of your Christmas decorations, or place them in your Advent prayer corner.

DECEMBER 11 ★ THIRD SUNDAY OF ADVENT

ISAIAH 35:1-6A, 10; JAMES 5:7-10; MATTHEW 11:2-11

Saints among us

"Among those born of women there has been none greater than John the Baptist; yet the least in the kingdom of heaven is greater than he."
MATTHEW 11:11

I met a saint a few months ago. She was about eight or nine years old and was receiving Holy Communion. When she knelt and gazed up at the host I held out for her, I felt caught up in eternity. I can't explain it, but I knew I was looking into the eyes of a saint. After Mass I happened to catch her mom and I told her about it. She laughed, giving me the impression her daughter was anything but saintly. But whether they've left their socks all over the living room or they're coming home too late at night, our children are all saints—no matter what we think. Jesus says it himself today. So how will you nurture your little saints today?

FAMILY PRAYER *(Based on Psalm 146)*

Parent: God is maker of heaven and earth.
   All: Alleluia!
Parent: He gives bread to the hungry and sight to the blind.
   All: Alleluia!
Parent: The Lord will reign forever through all generations.
   All: Alleluia!

(Light three candles on your Advent wreath, including the rose-colored one.)

ADVENT ACTION

Today is Gaudete Sunday. *Gaudete* means "rejoice" (which explains our rose candle). Together, create a "Reasons for Rejoicing" list.

DECEMBER 12 ★ MONDAY OF THE THIRD WEEK

ZECHARIAH 2:14-17 OR REVELATION 11:19A;12:1-6A, 10AB;
LUKE 1:26-38 OR LUKE 1:39-47

Hidden helper

A great sign appeared in the sky, a woman clothed with the sun, with the moon under her feet. REVELATION 12:1

A friend was going through a rough time supporting her adult son, who was fighting for custody of his child. One day, feeling the weight of her burden, she walked the hallway of the parish office where she works. Suddenly she stopped before a framed image of Our Lady of Guadalupe she'd never seen before. "Where did she come from?" she asked a coworker. The coworker was astonished. The image had hung there for years. My friend looked at the inscription (quoting what Mary said to St. Juan Diego): "Am I not here, I who am your mother?" That said it all. We might not notice, but Mary is always with us, quietly working and helping. How can Mary help you today?

FAMILY PRAYER

(Based on a prayer of St. John Paul II to Our Lady of Guadalupe)
Parent: Mary, hear our prayer and send it to your Son, Jesus.
   All: Mother Mary, hold us in your loving hands.
Parent: Mary, protect our family. Keep us united always.
   All: Mother Mary, hold us in your loving hands. Amen.

(Say a decade of the Rosary together.)

ADVENT ACTION

Celebrate Our Lady of Guadalupe, who is "clothed with the sun." Have an indoor picnic with sun- and moon-inspired foods like orange smoothies and gingersnaps dipped in white chocolate.

DECEMBER 13 ★ TUESDAY OF THE THIRD WEEK

ZEPHANIAH 3:1-2, 9-13; MATTHEW 21:28-32

Tough inside

"Yet even when you saw that, you did not later change your minds and believe him." MATTHEW 21:32

In the gospels, Jesus casts out many demons. But people with hard hearts? That's different. Remember the young man who tells Jesus he's followed all the commandments? When Jesus tells him to give away everything to the poor, he turns away from Jesus. Who's in worse shape? This law-abiding citizen, or the possessed youth in another passage who wildly thrashes about among the tombs? Even the demon submits to the power of God. But if my hard heart can't accept God's will, what will become of me? Please God, I may be a parent who knows the rules. But don't let me walk away from you. Pierce that armor of my self-protection. Save my soul.

FAMILY PRAYER

Parent: Lord Jesus, help us remember that in you there is no darkness.
   All: Light of the world, shine in me.
Parent: Jesus, guide us always by your light.
   All: Light of the world, shine in me.

(Pray silently for people who are blind to God's light.)

ADVENT ACTION

Celebrate St. Lucy's Day with kid-safe, Scandinavian candle wreaths. Cut out the center of a paper plate. Wrap the rim with green tissue paper. Twist four pieces of white tissue paper into candle shapes and color the ends orange. Glue to wreath and wear. As they say in Sweden, *God Jul!*

DECEMBER 14 ★ WEDNESDAY OF THE THIRD WEEK

ISAIAH 45:6B-8, 18, 21B-25; LUKE 7:18B-23

Age of offense

"And blessed is the one who takes no offense at me."
LUKE 7:23

The annual holiday assembly at my kids' public school celebrated many culture and faith traditions, from lighting menorahs to a St. Lucy's Day parade. It was canceled a few years ago when a parent protested, saying demonstrations of faith offended his child. I could be offended myself, but isn't being offended just a mature-sounding word for having a bit of a temper tantrum? And it's nothing new. Look at how many people were "offended" by Jesus. So what can modern Christians do in our easily offended age? We can decide we don't have time to be offended. Instead, we can spend our energy looking for Christ in everyone—even those who are offended by us.

FAMILY PRAYER

Parent: Lord God, bless the work we do.
   All: We praise you, O God.
Parent Help us do our jobs with happy hearts.
   All: We praise you, O God.
Parent: Let our work praise you, in the name of your Son, Jesus.
   All: We praise you, O God. Amen.

(Hold hands and say the Our Father together.)

ADVENT ACTION

Invite your friends and neighbors to share something about their family holiday traditions. Plan a relaxed get-together for after Christmas—to share these stories and photos.

DECEMBER 15 ★ THURSDAY OF THE THIRD WEEK

ISAIAH 54:1–10; LUKE 7:24–30

TGIF or TGIS

"Behold, I am sending my messenger ahead of you, he will prepare your way before you." LUKE 7:27

I heard a TED speaker explain that most people prefer Fridays over Sundays, even though Friday is a working day, and Sunday is dedicated to rest and worship. The speaker explained that on Friday we anticipate the weekend, while Sundays can find us dreading the coming week. I get that. We humans can get so busy looking ahead that we fail to see what's right in front of us. We might plan and save for the Ivy Leagues even though our daughter is unhappy in advanced math. We can look forward to the fullness of heaven but forget that God's kingdom is right here. Today, spend some time thinking about, well, today. Are you putting God off until tomorrow or helping create God's kingdom today?

FAMILY PRAYER

Parent: Father, you sent John into the wilderness to prepare people's hearts for your Son.
   All: Prepare the way of the Lord.
Parent: Help us hear John's words and turn from sin.
   All: Prepare the way of the Lord.
Parent: Help us see your ways clearly, O Lord.
   All: Prepare the way of the Lord. Amen.

(Pray silently with hands on your hearts to show that you're preparing for the Lord.)

ADVENT ACTION

Make John the Baptist snacks. Top carrots and celery with peanut or almond butter and honey. Sprinkle with raisins (locusts) and enjoy.

DECEMBER 16 ★ FRIDAY OF THE THIRD WEEK

ISAIAH 56:1-3A, 6-8; JOHN 5:33-36

Coming home

Let not the foreigner say, when he would join himself to the Lord, "The Lord will surely exclude me from his people." **Isaiah 56:3**

My friend's three-year-old singlehandedly cleared an entire church pew in fifteen seconds when his morning oatmeal made an encore appearance. My friend was so embarrassed it took months before she could return to Mass. Bringing kids to church isn't easy, but they need it, we need it, and so does every other person there. We need to hear crying babies to remind us that taking up Jesus' cross can be painful. We need to see kids getting distracted because, by golly, we get distracted too. We need other families to remind us that we all get sick, run late, and feel unworthy. Bring the kids to Mass, because none of us is perfect—that's why we're there.

FAMILY PRAYER

All: Good Jesus, thank you for calling me here to be with you. I believe that you are present here in the Blessed Sacrament in a special, holy way. I love you with all of my heart. Amen.

(Say this prayer quietly with your children at church.)

ADVENT ACTION

Raise your kids' comfort level at Mass by visiting church on a weekday. Be reverent, but let them lead the exploring. Let them touch statues (carefully) and sit wherever they want. Show them how Jesus is present in the tabernacle.

DECEMBER 17 ★ SATURDAY OF THE THIRD WEEK
GENESIS 49:2, 8-10; MATTHEW 1:1-17

Family values

Thus the total number of generations from Abraham to David is fourteen generations... **Matthew 1:17**

Matthew begins his gospel with a list of Jesus' ancestors in order to show his audience how Jesus is their long-awaited Messiah, descending directly from Abraham and David. It's uplifting to be part of history; that's why family traditions are so important. Today, a prayer tradition dating from the eighth century begins, but it's easy to miss. The "O" Antiphons are part of the Liturgy of the Hours and speak of Old Testament hopes for the Messiah. You hear their echoes in each day's Mass reading and in the Alleluia verse before the gospel, where a different title for Jesus is offered—Key of David, Root of Jesse, and more. The titles and antiphons are steeped in history and meaning. They are a deep part of us all.

FAMILY PRAYER

Parent: O come, Emmanuel, Prince of Peace.
    All: O come, O come, Emmanuel.
Parent: Come, O Wisdom from on high, show us the path of knowledge.
    All: O come, O come, Emmanuel.
Parent: Rejoice! Emmanuel shall come to us, O Israel.
    All: O come, O come, Emmanuel. Amen.

(Invite a family member to sing this hymn if they know it.)

ADVENT ACTION

Challenge your kids to find the O antiphon symbols for Jesus (Emmanuel, Key of David, etc.) in each day's Mass readings until Christmas. Find the daily readings at usccb.org.

DECEMBER 18 ★ FOURTH SUNDAY OF ADVENT

ISAIAH 7:10-14; ROMANS 1:1-7; MATTHEW 1:18-24

Rest reasons

The angel of the Lord appeared to him in a dream and said, "Joseph, son of David, do not be afraid to take Mary your wife into your home."
MATTHEW 1:20

Because running away from you is their favorite activity. Because they make at least three wardrobe changes a day. Because they can do everything themselves. Because they need you—and only you—in the middle of the night. They're just a few of the reasons you're exhausted right now, but they're also the reasons you need to make rest a priority. Think sleep is a luxury for parents? Ponder this. What would have become of Joseph's family if he hadn't slept? He received God's lifesaving messages in his dreams. Don't be the parent who misses God's messages, at least today. Get some rest. What might God be trying to tell you?

FAMILY PRAYER

Parent: Lord God, bless our sleep tonight.
   All: Good night, dear Jesus.
Parent: Guard our dreams and keep us close to you.
   All: Good night, dear Jesus.
Parent: Give us peace and strength to meet another day.
   All: Good night, dear Jesus. Amen.

(Light all four candles on your Advent wreath and pray for God's peace to reign in your house.)

ADVENT ACTION

Put some play in your rest. Make a blanket fort together, and read stories from a children's Bible or saints book.

DECEMBER 19 ★ MONDAY OF THE FOURTH WEEK

JUDGES 13:2-7, 24-25A; LUKE 1:5-25

Chance encounter

*He was chosen by lot to enter the sanctuary
of the Lord to burn incense.*

LUKE 1:9

Zechariah is chosen "by lot" to be the one in the sanctuary on this particular day. Isn't it interesting how random events can suddenly converge to reveal the hand of God? I'm sure I've failed to recognize these moments throughout my life. Maybe you have too. But we can't feel too bad. Even someone like Zechariah, a mature, holy man with lots of experience, missed the message until it was almost too late. Still, God gave Zechariah a second chance. Have there been any opportunities you've missed this year? Is God inviting you to learn something from them? Or is he offering you a second chance? Find out by spending time with him today.

FAMILY PRAYER

Parent: Mighty God, help us listen when you speak to us.
   All: Your words are spirit and life.
Parent: Powerful God, help us listen when others speak.
   All: Your words are spirit and life.
Parent: Great God, help us wait before we speak, especially in anger or impatience.
   All: Your words are spirit and life. Amen.

(Say the guardian angel prayer together.)

ADVENT ACTION

Make angel cards. Trace kids' handprints (both hands, spread out) on colored paper. Glue a picture of your child in the center. Add lines, if needed. Fold and use as thank-you notes after Christmas.

DECEMBER 20 ★ TUESDAY OF THE FOURTH WEEK

ISAIAH 7:10-14; LUKE 1:26-38

Signs of life

"Therefore the Lord himself will give you this sign: the virgin shall conceive and bear a son, and shall name him Emmanuel." Isaiah 7:14

For most of us, there will be no mighty angels. No portents in the heavens, no lightning or thunder. The cameras won't roll; the orchestra won't cue up. For us, the signs of God's presence might be as subtle as a flickering candle or as soft as a baby's head. God calls us so gently. And the way we hear God today may be vastly different from how we heard him ten years ago. The secret to keeping our joy is to remain open to God's message at every stage of our life. Just because we're adults, just because we went to Catholic school, just because we might teach kids ourselves, it doesn't mean we stop listening for and learning from God. What are God's signs to you today?

FAMILY PRAYER *(Speak in a whisper.)*
Parent: Jesus, we look forward to your birth in the stable.
   All: Silent night, holy night.
Parent: Draw us close to you, where all is calm and bright.
   All: Silent night, holy night.
Parent: Help us be gentle and mild with each other right now.
   All: Sleep in heavenly peace! Amen.

(Have everyone whisper a prayer intention.)

ADVENT ACTION
Take a video of your family singing a Christmas carol by candlelight.

DECEMBER 21 ★ WEDNESDAY OF THE FOURTH WEEK

SONG OF SONGS 2:8-14 OR ZEPHANIAH 3:14-18A; LUKE 1:39-45

Garden season

The flowers appear on the earth, the time of pruning the vines has come, and the song of the dove is heard in our land. SONG OF SONGS 2:12

"Aslan is on the move!" Today's passage from the Song of Songs reminds me of *The Lion, the Witch and the Wardrobe*. In C.S. Lewis's allegorical tale, the land of Narnia is under the spell of the White Witch, so it's always winter and never Christmas. But at the approach of Aslan, the magnificent lion and Narnia's real ruler, the snow melts and spring returns. On this first day of winter, flowers feel out of place—until we remember that our Savior is on the move. God has promised that he will save us from sin and death. Our winter may seem endless, but spring will return, as surely as Jesus brings life to us all.

FAMILY PRAYER

Parent: Lord God, thank you for this winter season.
   All: Keep your people safe, Lord.
Parent: Watch over us, Lord, in all kinds of weather.
   All: Keep your people safe, Lord.
Parent: Help us remember those who need warmth and shelter.
   All: Keep your people safe, Lord. Amen.

(Pray for those who need help this winter, especially the homeless and elderly.)

ADVENT ACTION

Collect coats, hats, and other winter clothing that your kids have outgrown, and donate to a homeless shelter.

DECEMBER 22 ★ THURSDAY OF THE FOURTH WEEK

1 SAMUEL 1:24-28; LUKE 1:46-56

Guide to feasting

"He has filled the hungry with good things, and the rich he has sent away empty." LUKE 1:53

God certainly fills us with good things this time of year: there's that gift basket full of candy someone left in the conference room, and all those Starbucks cards you've received—enough to keep you caffeinated until March. And don't forget the neighborhood potluck and the holiday breakfast, brunch, lunch, and dinner dates you've made. If you've been going to bed feeling uncomfortably full lately, or you're unhappy with your eating choices, don't beat yourself up. Instead, read Mary's Magnificat slowly and prayerfully today. Let this prayer be your guide through these coming days of feasting and celebration.

FAMILY PRAYER *(Based on Mary's Magnificat)*

Parent: We proclaim the greatness of the Lord, rejoicing in God our Savior.
  All: Holy is his name.
Parent: The Almighty has done great things for us. His mercy is on those who love him in every generation.
  All: Holy is his name.
Parent: He has remembered his promise to our fathers, to Abraham and his children forever.
  All: Holy is his name. Amen.

(Read the Magnificat [Luke 1:46-55] in place of grace tonight.)

ADVENT ACTION

Find out which items are really needed at your local food bank; if you are able, go shopping with your family for nonperishables to donate.

DECEMBER 23 ★ FRIDAY OF THE FOURTH WEEK
MALACHI 3:1-4, 23-24; LUKE 1:57-66

Guest of honor

But who will endure the day of his coming?
MALACHI 3:2

How will you endure the day of your Christmas visitors' coming? And all the exhausting days that follow? And what if you're the visitor, planning a long car trip or plane ride with kids in tow? First remember that overly high expectations will disrupt your family's Christmas peace faster than King Herod could lose his temper. So realistically look at your plans today and decide what you can and can't do. If you're having guests, don't try to run a five-star hotel. If you're traveling, expect that your kids will get tired and cranky. Ask Mary to wrap you in her mantle of love, and you will come and go with God's grace.

FAMILY PRAYER

Parent: Lord God, we remember that Mary and Joseph found no room in the inn. But we want to make room for all. So help us, Lord. It may get uncomfortable; we may get squished or bumped or forgotten about sometimes. But help us remember that you are present in our guests and fellow travelers. Help us see you wherever we go.

All: Help us make room, Lord Jesus, for you. Amen.

(Together discuss how it might have felt for Mary and Joseph to find shelter in a stable.)

ADVENT ACTION

Have your kids write or draw lists of your guests' or hosts' favorite things so they have some conversation starters in advance of visits.

DECEMBER 24 ★ SATURDAY OF THE FOURTH WEEK

2 SAMUEL 7:1-5, 8B-12, 14A, 16; LUKE 1:67-79

Wrap it up

Zechariah his father, filled with the Holy Spirit, prophesied...
LUKE 1:67

I know you're busy today, so I'll make this quick. A few days ago we saw Zechariah acting like a typical sitcom dad, not getting the message. Today, he's filled with the Holy Spirit and prophesying. What a transformation! Only God can do that kind of work. So whatever you didn't get done, whatever Advent activities you missed, don't worry about it too much. God has transformed you this season—through his own power and love and through his gift of your beautiful children. All you have to do is look in their eyes today and you'll know it's true.

FAMILY PRAYER

Parent: Father in heaven, bless this beautiful tree.
All: God bless all of us.
Parent: Let its fresh branches remind us of our new life in your Son, Jesus.
All: God bless all of us.
Parent: Let the gifts we place here remind us that Jesus is the best gift of all.
All: God bless all of us. Amen.

(*Gather around your tree and marvel at the beauty of God's creation.*)

ADVENT ACTION

Read a Christmas story to your kids by the light of your tree.